20 Super Easy Piano Pieces
on the Black Keys

Composed by Giovanni Andreani

Illustrated by Greta Scainelli

First published in 2021 by
GA
Via Colombo 4, 24061 Albano Sant'Alessandro, BG, Italy
Copyright © Giovanni Andreani 2016
ISBN 978-88-941122-3-8

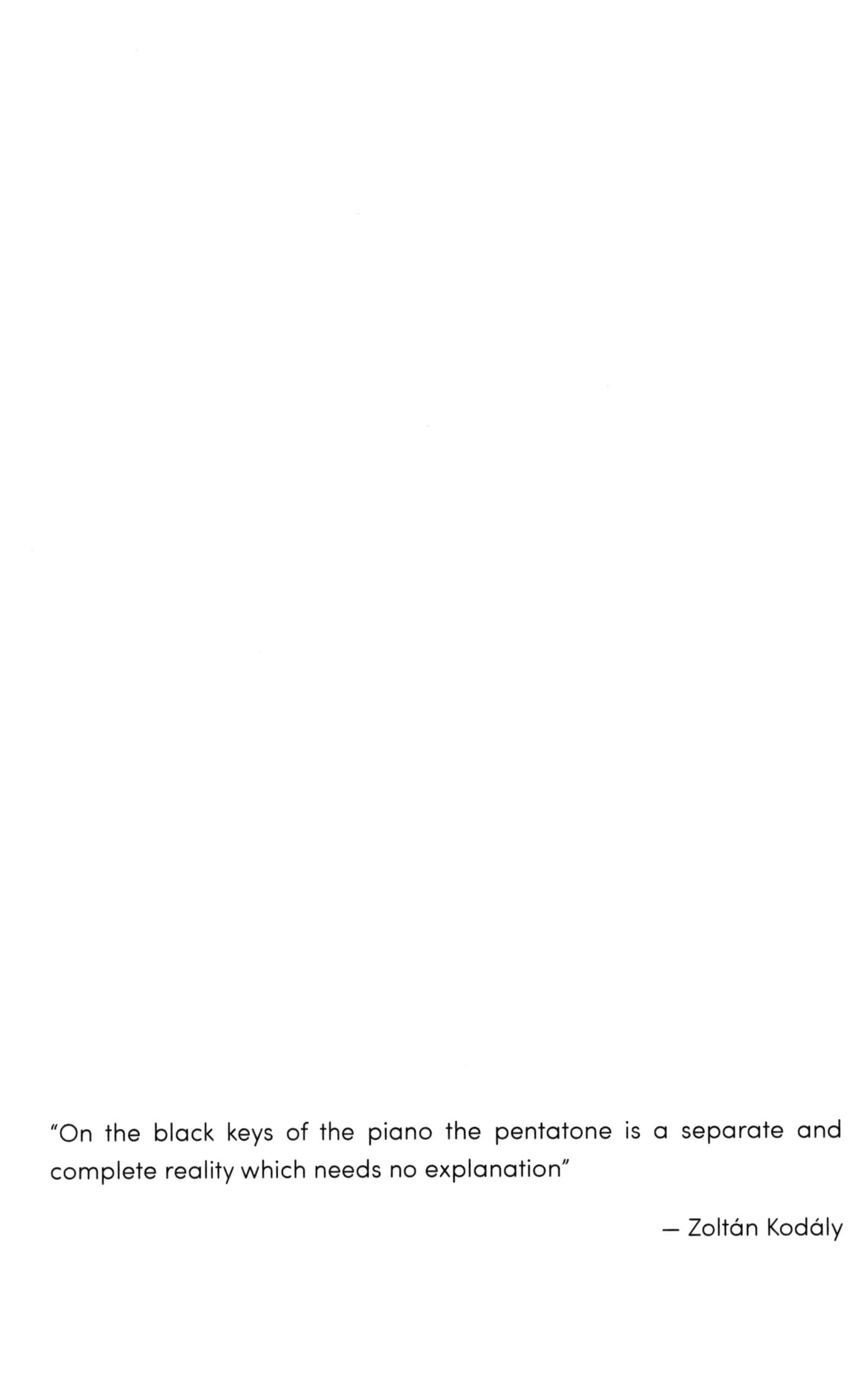

"On the black keys of the piano the pentatone is a separate and complete reality which needs no explanation"

— Zoltán Kodály

INTRODUCTION

There are many reasons for considering playing only on the black keys at a very early stage. In 1945, Zoltan Kodály said: 'Piano playing should be started on the black keys. On them the penta-tone appears as a separate, closed system which need not be extracted from the heptatone as if it were something gap-toothed, incomplete. Misgivings about fingering are quickly dispersed by anyone who tries it seriously.'

These 20 pieces are 'super easy' because they don't require simultaneous coordination between the two hands. The melody, by constantly passing from one hand to the other, will encourage a sharper ability to control the shape of a melodic profile that is different when compared with two hands playing simultaneously and the theme constantly being played by the same hand. However, two pieces – 'Looking at the Milky Way' and 'The Magic Island' – require further control for a short stretch in which the two hands will be playing together; furthermore, in 'The Chinese Factory', which is – among all the pieces – the most challenging, the two hands are required to play together throughout the entire piece.

20 Super Easy Piano Pieces on the Black Keys is a collection of small canvases characterised by fitting a musical guise to each of them. Each piece – accompanied by an illustration – is presented with a title that can serve as a guide to the most effective performance. In this way, the performer will be able to project him/herself into the appropriate imaginary dimension necessary for achieving a compelling and persuasive performance. Technical skills will then naturally increase in a surprising way.

Of all the pieces, the following two require further description to enable their most effective performance.

'My Dad Got Rid of that Monster under My Bed'

In this piece, the left hand represents the monster, the right hand a little boy (or girl). A little boy is under his bed sheets, on the verge of falling asleep, when he has a feeling that a scary creature is lurking under his bed (mm. 1–2). Intimidated, he huddles under the sheets (mm. 3–4) while the haunting creature makes its presence clearly evident (mm. 5–6). The little boy is certain that it's a fearsome creature and he tries to make himself even smaller (mm. 7–8). Unfortunately, the dreadful presence seems to want to creep out from under the bed (mm. 9–10). The little boy wants to call for help, but he just whispers, fearing that the monster will immediately detect him; he then tries to shrink himself as small as a dot and closes his eyes tightly (mm. 11–12). The monster finally decides to come out into the open, exhibiting his full viciousness (mm. 13–14). The little boy's father – who thinks he hears his child's soft voice calling for help – is nearby and, without hesitation, he strikes the monster's head with four powerful punches (mm. 15–17, played by thumping the keys with the closed fist of the right hand). The monster can't be heard anymore; all is quiet (m. 18). Mortified by the rounds sustained, the monster silently disappears (mm. 19–20), never to be seen again (m. 21).

'The Chinese Factory'

In this piece, the left hand represents the factory's mechanical arms and marks the start of a new incessant working day by hammering the keys with the fist, positioned as if holding a Sky Stick. The first two measures should be played continuously, starting very slowly while gradually increasing the speed until the required tempo is reached, highlighting a characteristic of unceasing heaviness, establishing the beginning of the day's work. The last two measures should be played as if summoning the gradual phasing-out of all the machinery, until the last cog has stopped moving.

INTRODUZIONE

Vi sono molti motivi per considerare di suonare sui tasti neri sin da un primissimo livello. Zoltan Kodály, nel 1945, affermò: "Si dovrebbe iniziare a suonare il pianoforte dai tasti neri. Dalla loro disposizione, la struttura pentatonica appare come un sistema chiuso e distinguibile e non come la parte incompleta del sistema eptatonico da cui è estratta. Con un approccio attento, le perplessità sulla diteggiatura svaniscono rapidamente".

Questi 20 brani sono 'super easy' perché non impegnano simultaneamente le due mani. La melodia, passando continuamente da una mano all'altra, svilupperà una più spiccata capacità di controllo della linea melodica rispetto ad un'esecuzione in cui le due mani suonassero simultaneamente, col tema eseguito costantemente dalla stessa mano. Vi sono tuttavia due brani, 'Looking at the Milky Way' e 'The Magic Island', in cui è richiesta - per un breve tratto - una coordinazione e controllo d'esecuzione simultanea delle due mani, mentre nell'ultimo brano 'The Chinese Factory' - che tra tutti è il più impegnativo - le due mani suoneranno simultaneamente da capo a fondo.

20 Super Easy Piano Pieces on the Black Keys consiste in una raccolta di piccoli quadri a cui attribuire una veste sonora che li caratterizzi efficacemente. Guidato dal titolo e dall'illustrazione, l'interprete potrà proiettarsi nella dimensione immaginifica necessaria per raggiungere un'interpretazione convincente e persuasiva. In tal modo, la tecnica - di volta in volta necessaria all'esecuzione - maturerà più spontaneamente di quanto non ci si possa attendere.

Fra tutti i brani, i due seguenti necessitano di una particolare descrizione a favore di una più efficace interpretazione:

'My Dad Got Rid of that Monster under My Bed'

In questo brano, la mano sinistra rappresenta un mostro e la mano destra un bambino (o una bambina). Un bimbo cerca di addormentarsi ma ha la sensazione che sotto il suo letto si annidi un'inquietante presenza (miss. 1-2). Intimorito, si rannicchia sotto le coperte (miss. 3-4), mentre l'inquietante presenza si rende più evidente (miss. 5-6). Il bimbo è certo che si tratti di una creatura spaventosa e cerca di farsi ancora più piccolo (miss. 7-8); purtroppo, la creatura spaventosa sembra proprio intenzionata a rendere manifeste le proprie intenzioni (miss. 9-10). Il bimbo prova quindi a chiedere aiuto: lo fa pianissimo perché ha paura che il mostro - sentendolo - lo individui immediatamente; allora cerca di farsi piccolo come un puntino e chiude stretti gli occhi (miss. 11-12), nella speranza di passare inosservato. Il mostro decide di uscire allo scoperto esibendo tutta la sua cattiveria (miss. 13-14). Il papà del bimbo - a cui era sembrato di sentire, pianissimo, la voce del figlio chiedere aiuto - si trova proprio lì vicino e senza indugio, sferra quattro pugni sulla testa della spaventosa creatura, potenti come mazzuolate (miss.15-17, suonando i tasti col pugno della mano destra). Il mostro non si sente più, tutto tace (mis. 18). Mortificato per la scarica subita, silenziosamente si dissolve (miss. 19-20), scomparendo nel nulla, per sempre (mis. 21).

'The Chinese Factory'

In questo brano, la mano sinistra rappresenta le braccia meccaniche che nella fabbrica segnalano l'inizio dell'incessante lavoro quotidiano, percuotendo i tasti con la parte esterna della mano chiusa con le dita piegate e strette sul palmo a formare un pugno, nella stessa posizione come per afferrare una racchetta da sci. Le prime due misure devono essere continuamente suonate iniziando lentissimamente fino a raggiungere il tempo richiesto, evidenziando un carattere di incessante pesantezza, a sancire l'inizio della giornata di lavoro. Le ultime due misure devono essere suonate evocando lo spegnimento graduale di tutti i macchinari, sino a quando l'ultimo ingranaggio non avrà smesso di funzionare.

GA 19028

CONTENTS

GA 19028

Waking Up

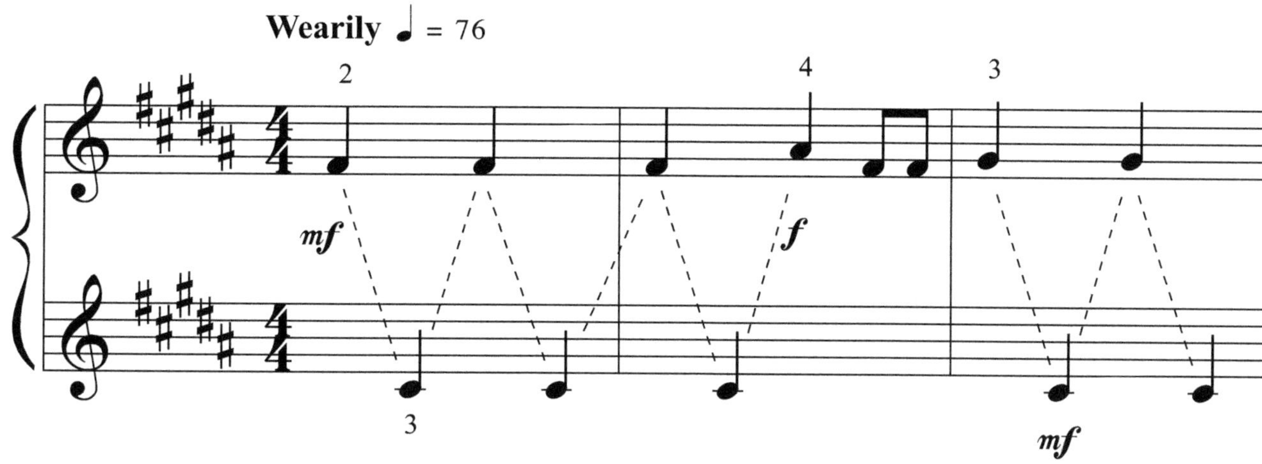

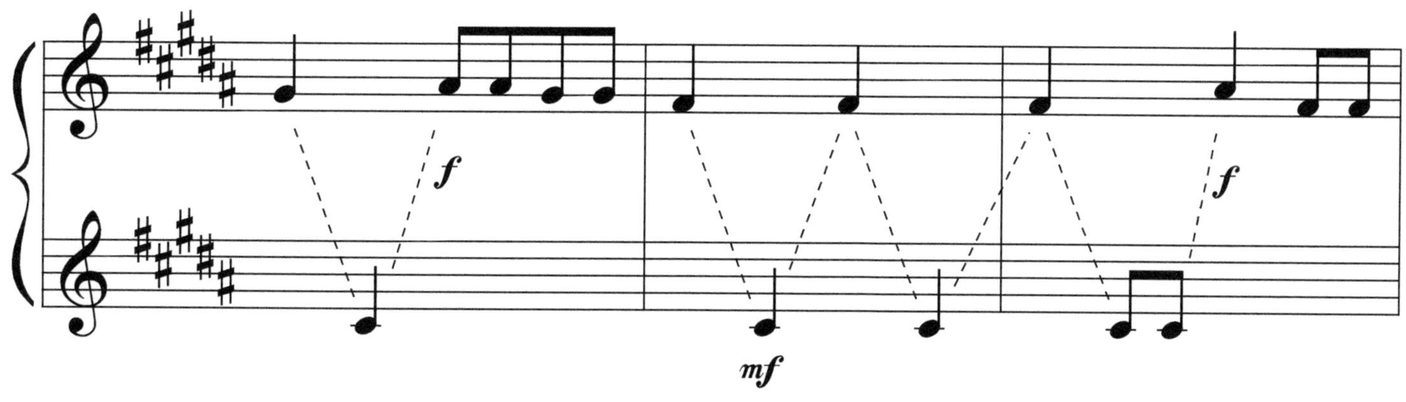

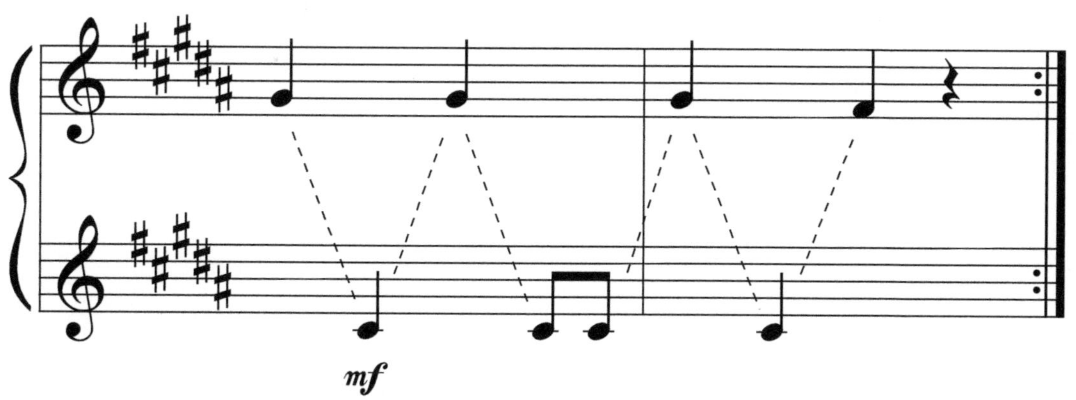

GA 19028

1

Walking My Dog

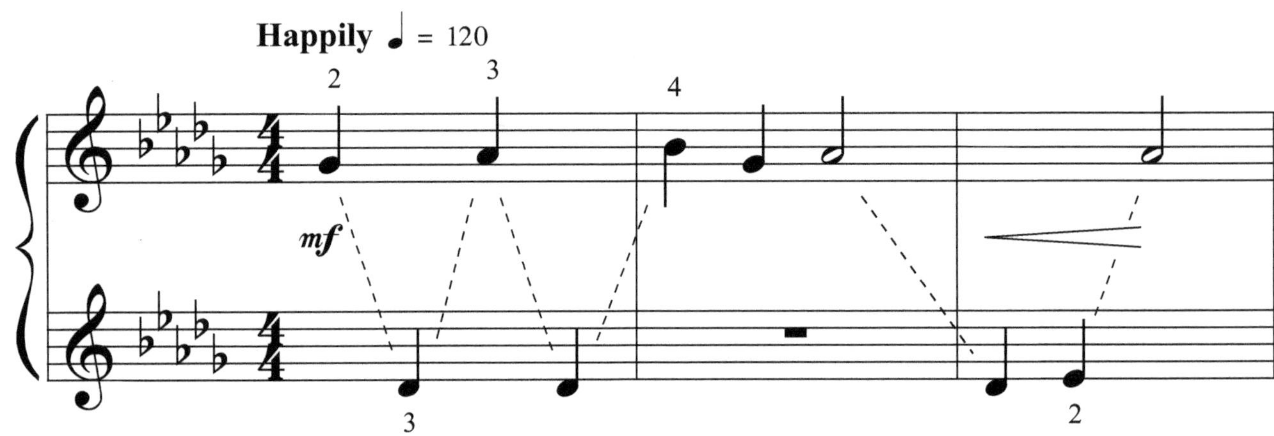

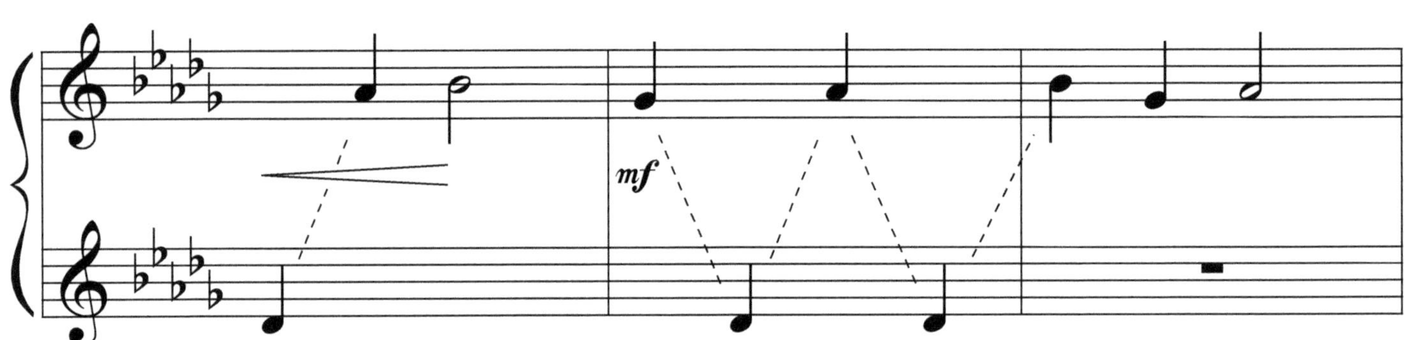

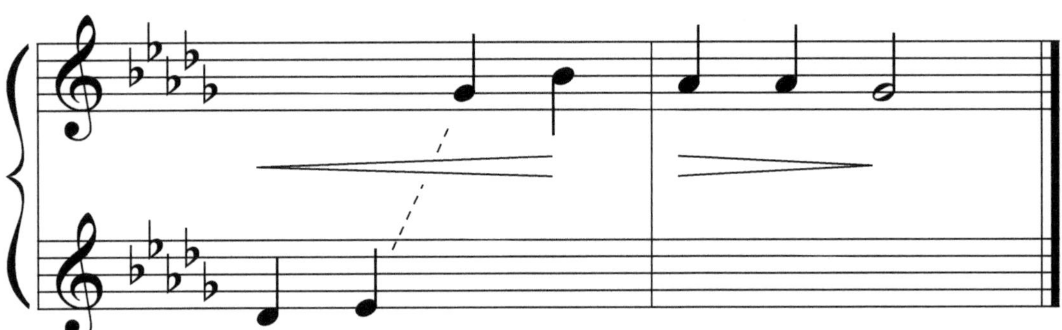

GA 19028

GA 19028

Waving to My Friend

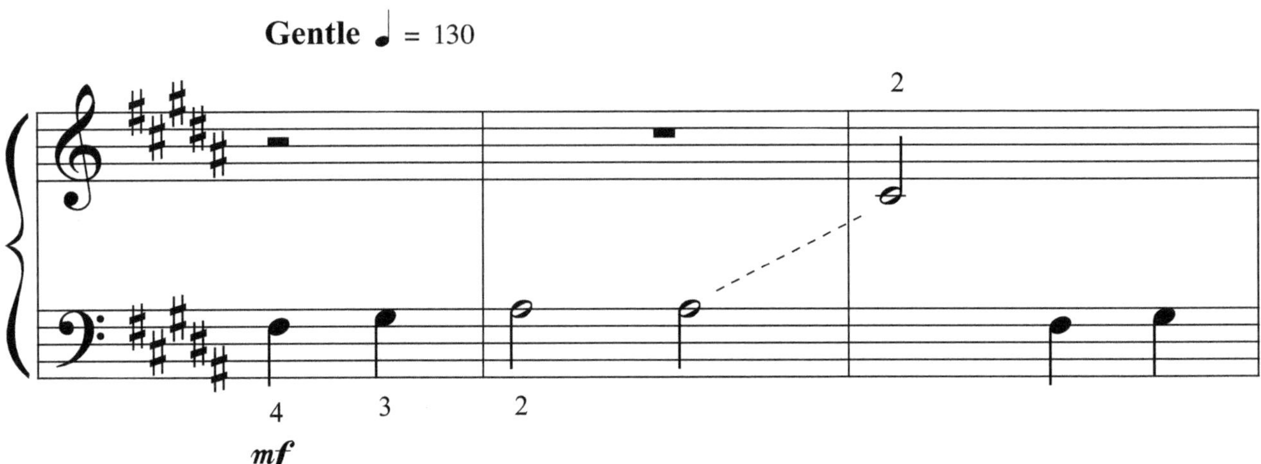

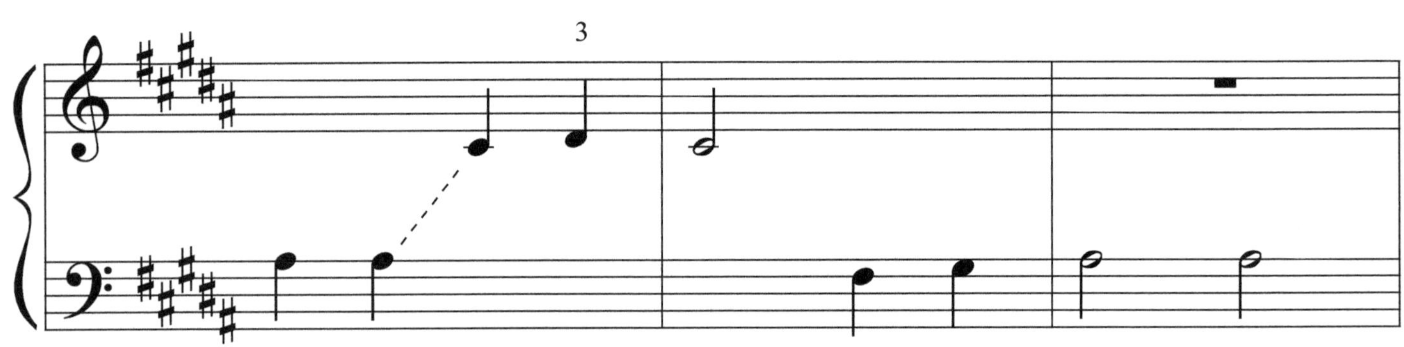

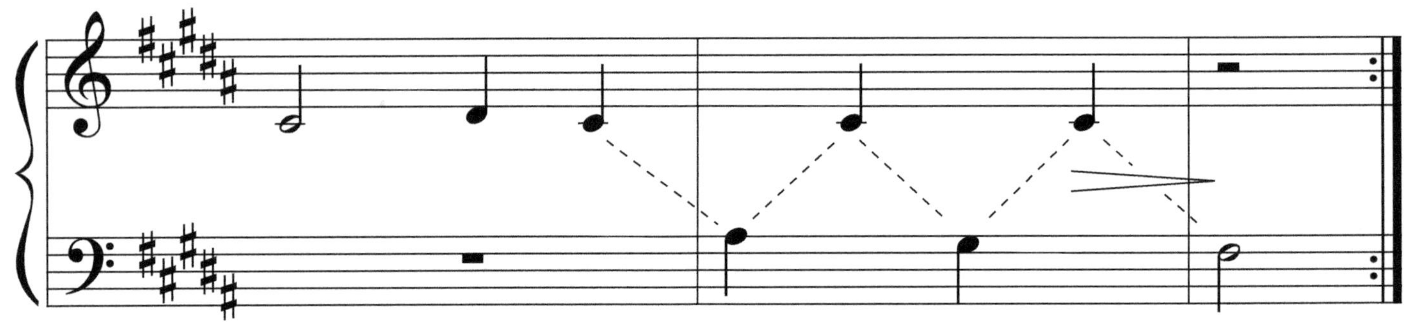

GA 19028

The Windmill

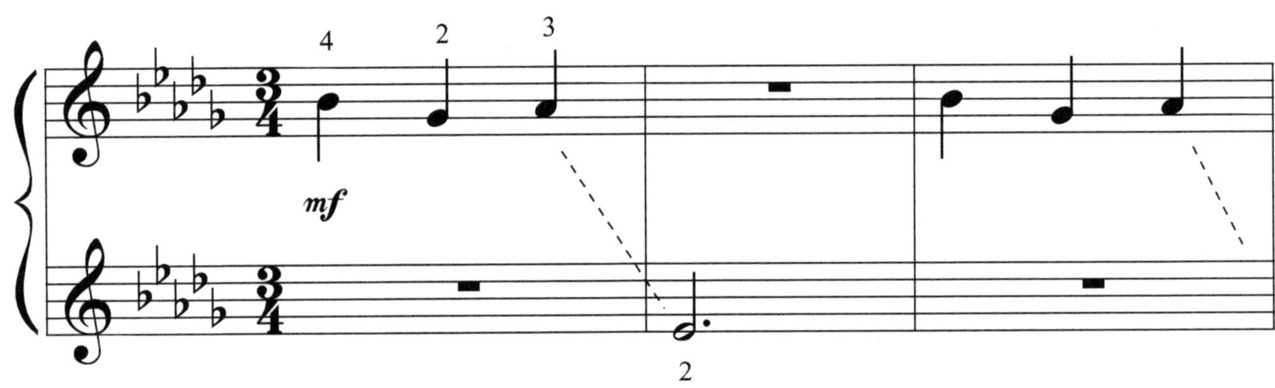

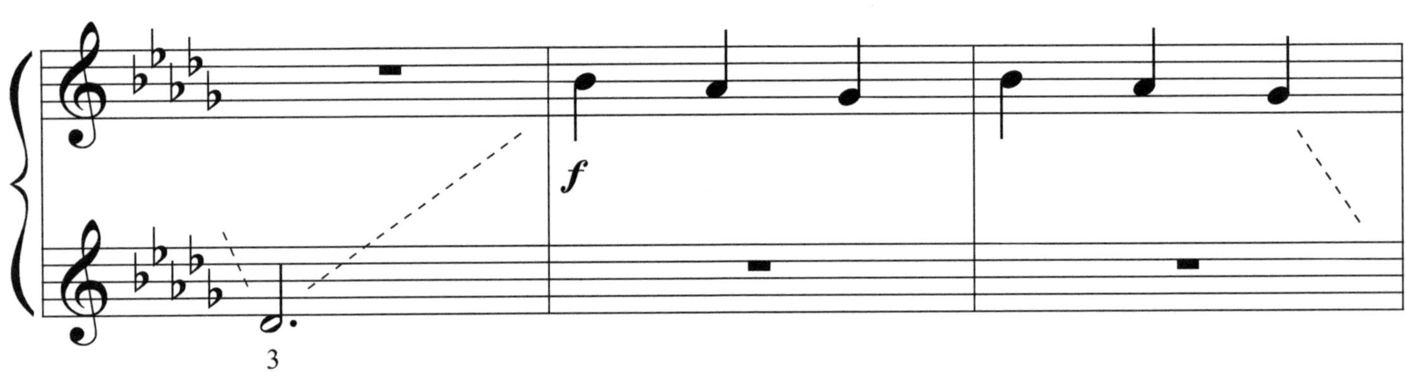

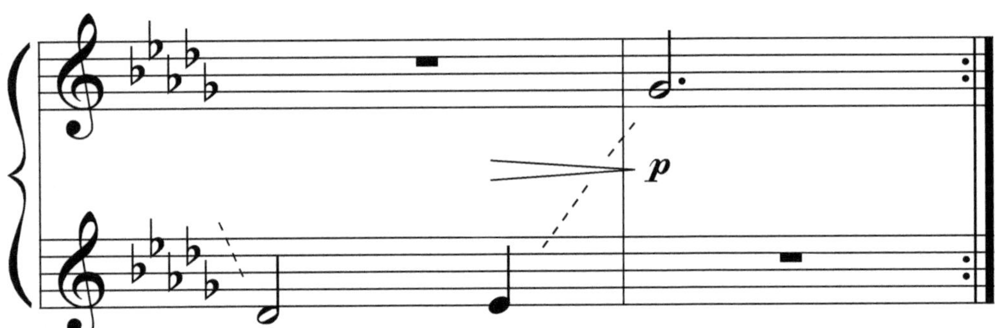

GA 19028

GA 19028

Pony Ride

With a moderate trot ♩ = 96

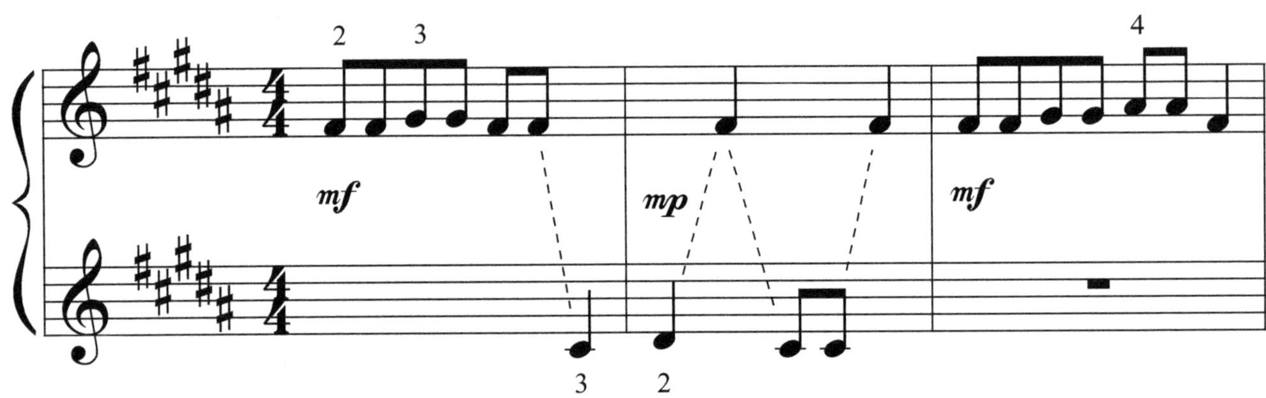

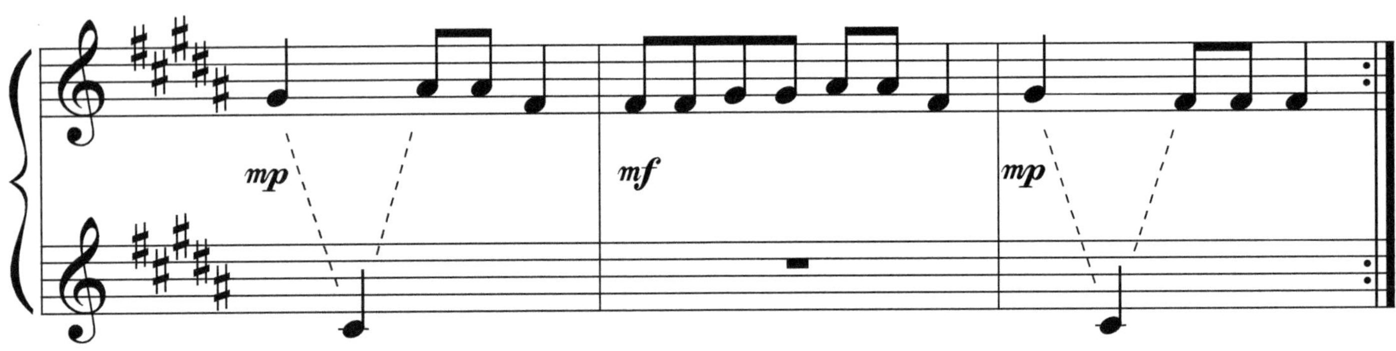

GA 19028

Around the Pond

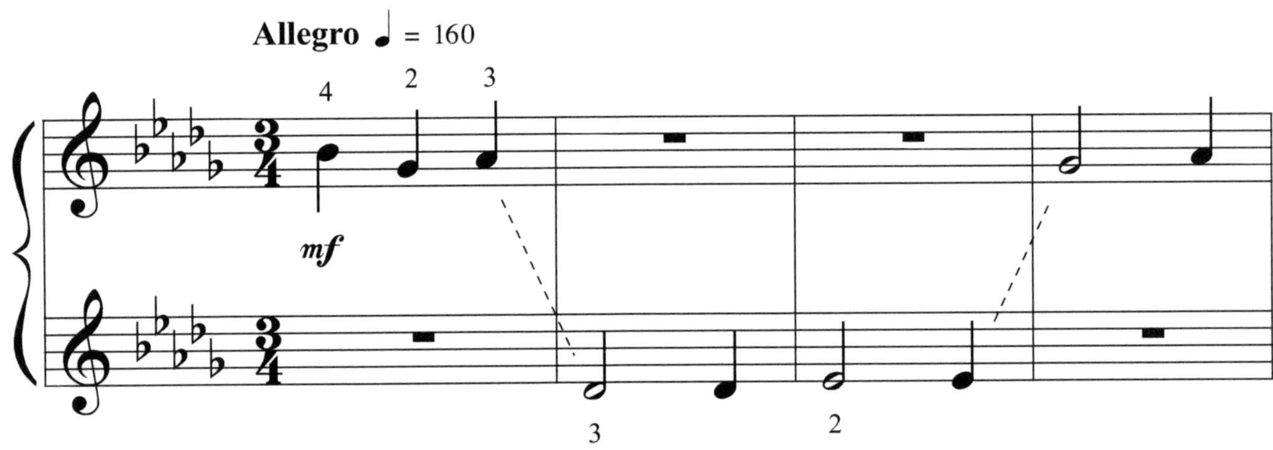

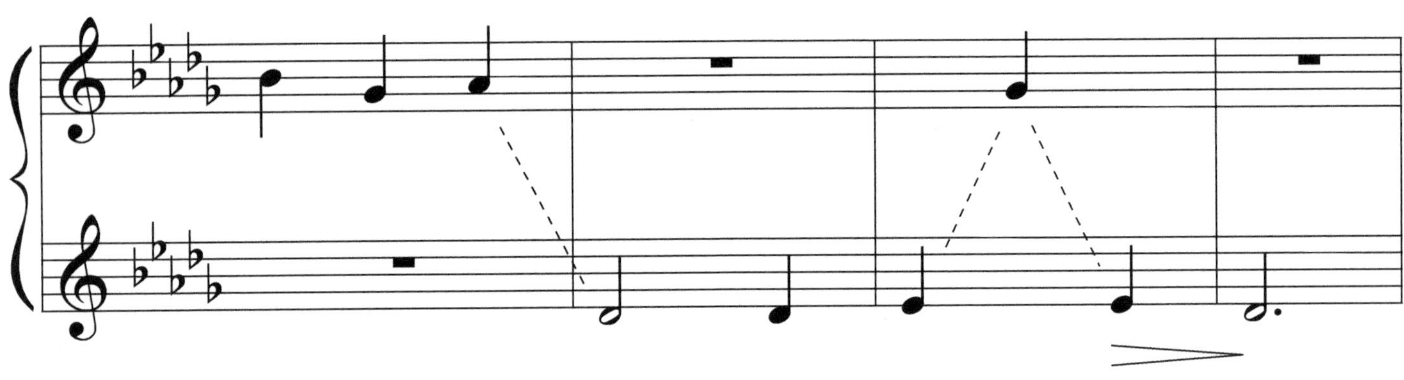

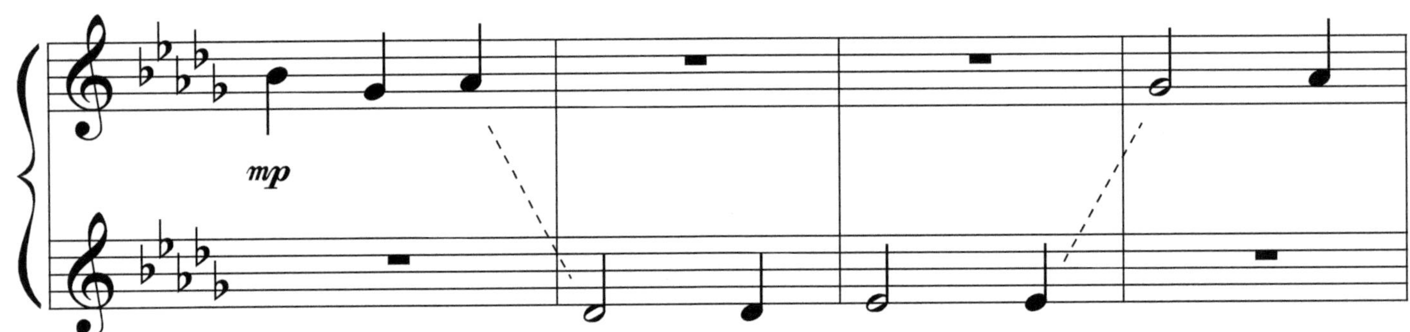

GA 19028

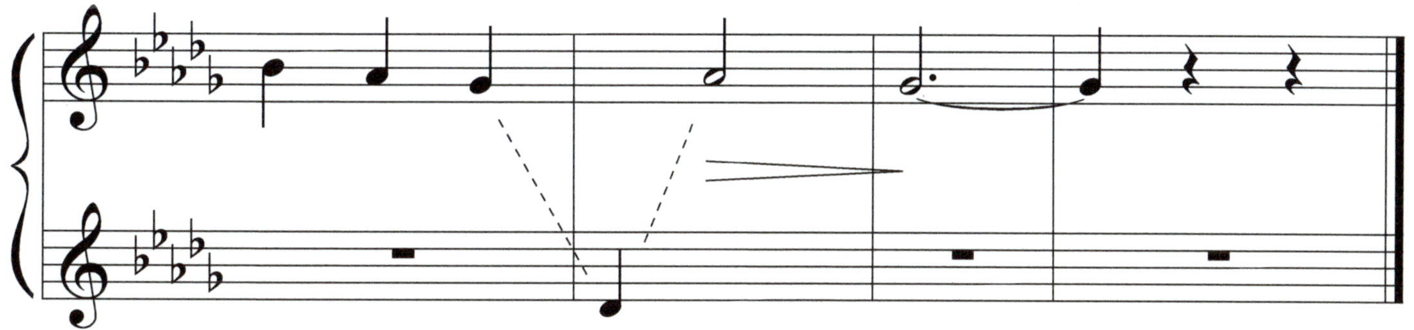

The Woodpecker

GA 19028

A Busy Day!

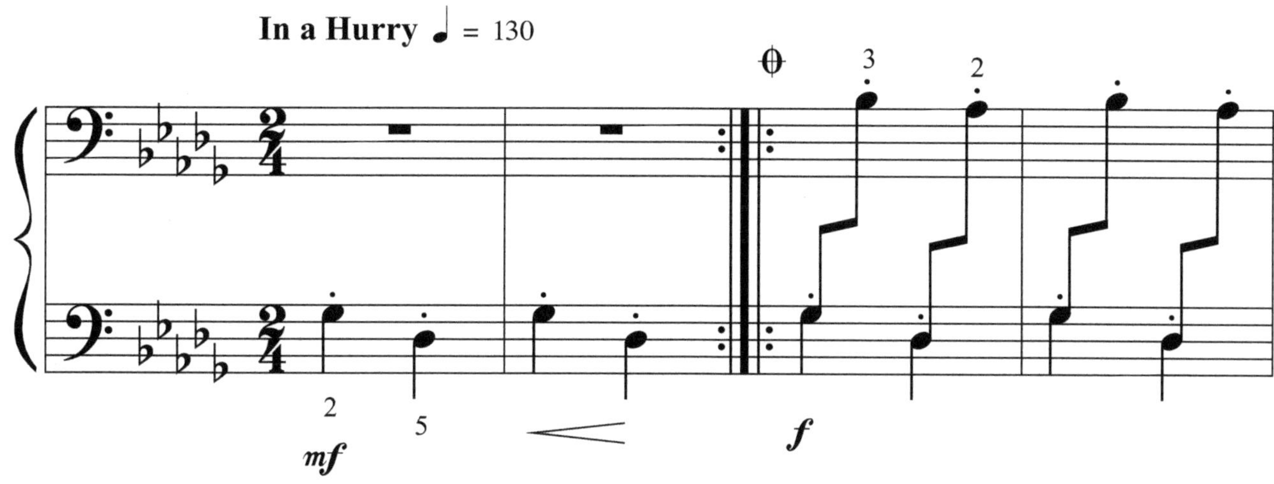

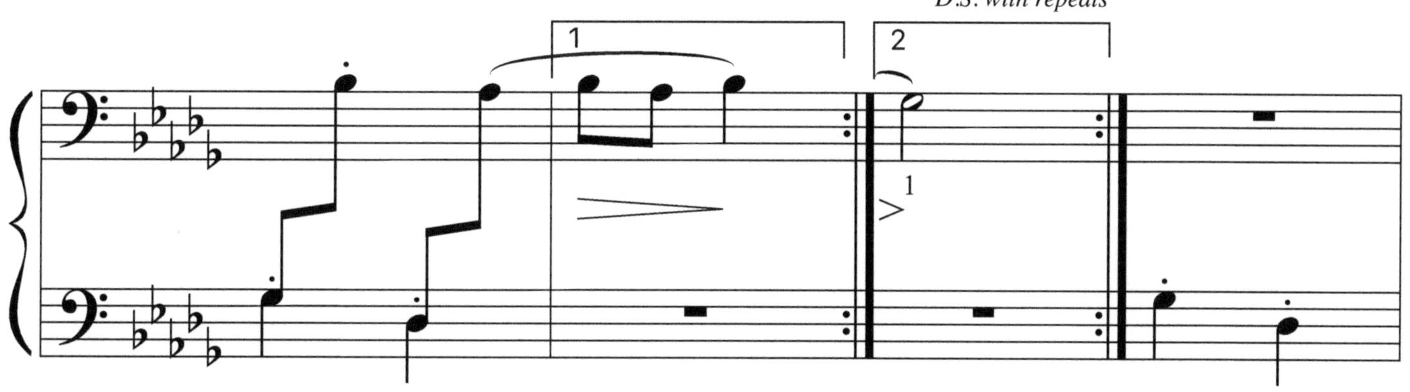

Walking on the Hills

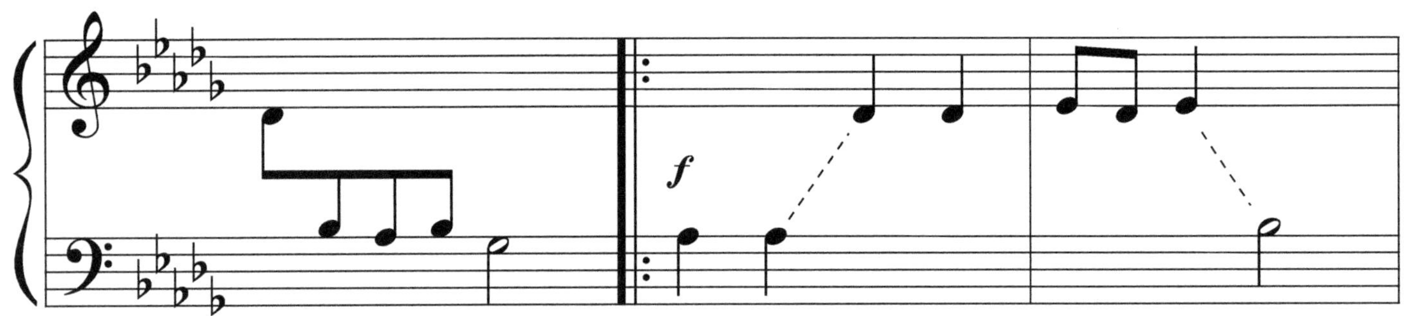

GA 19028

GA 19028

The Elephant Goes to Market

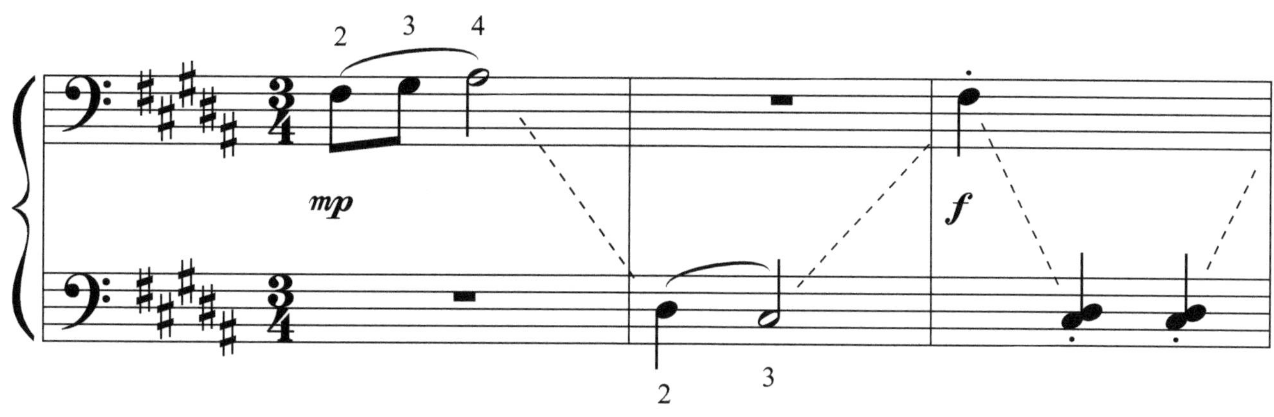

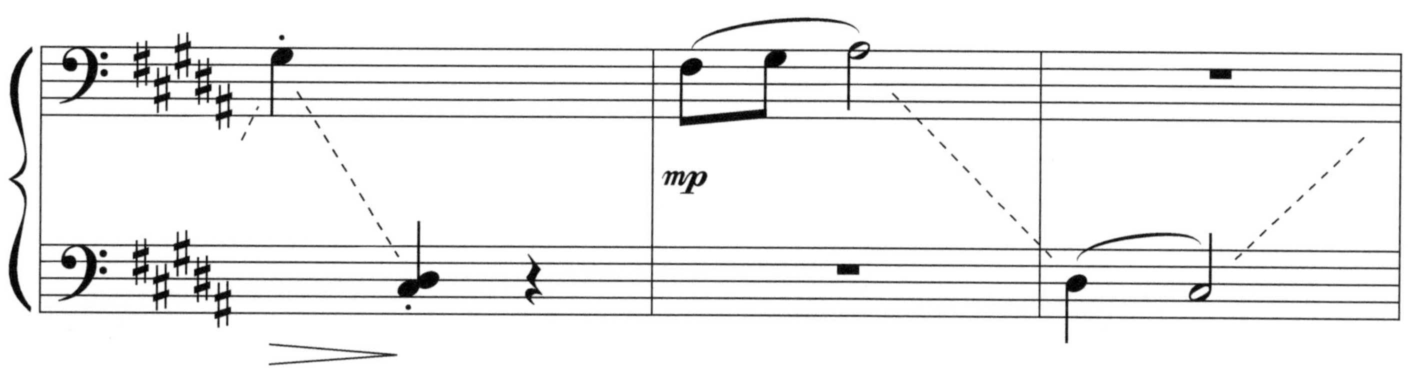

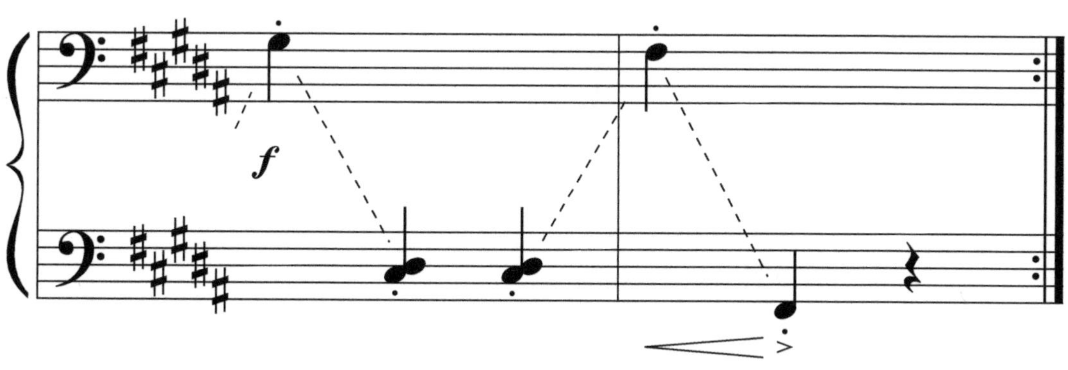

Looking at the Milky Way

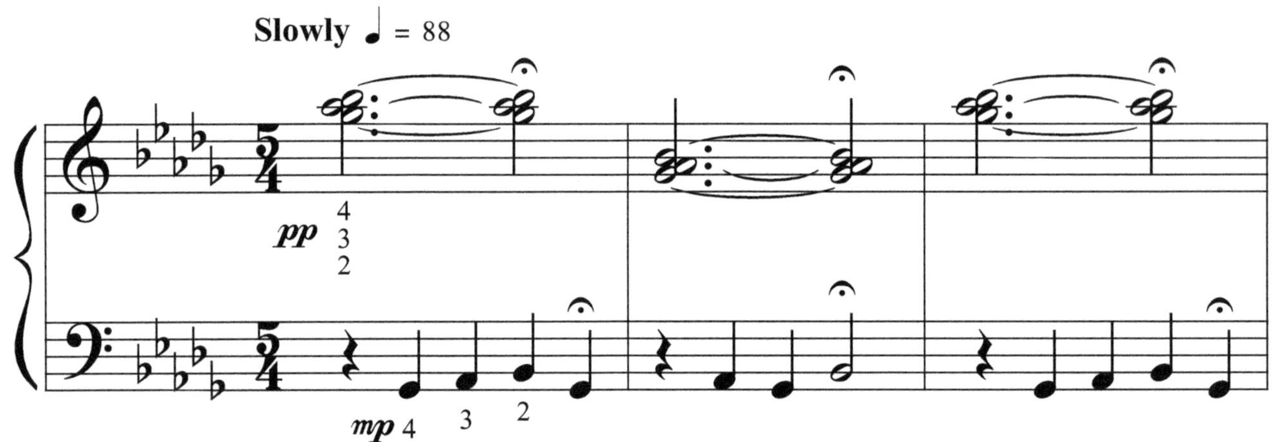

GA 19028

The Mechanical Clock

Mechanically ♩ = 120

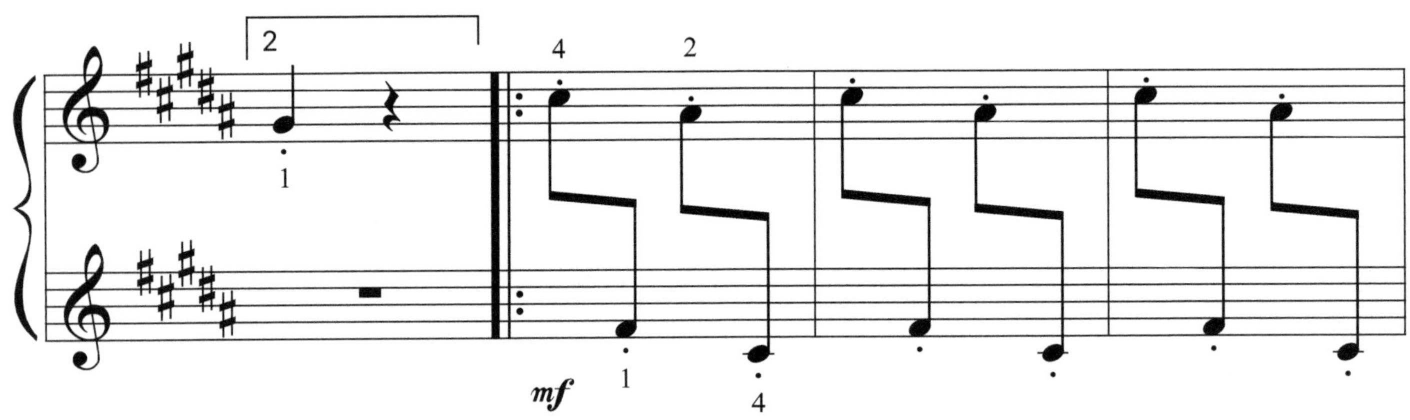

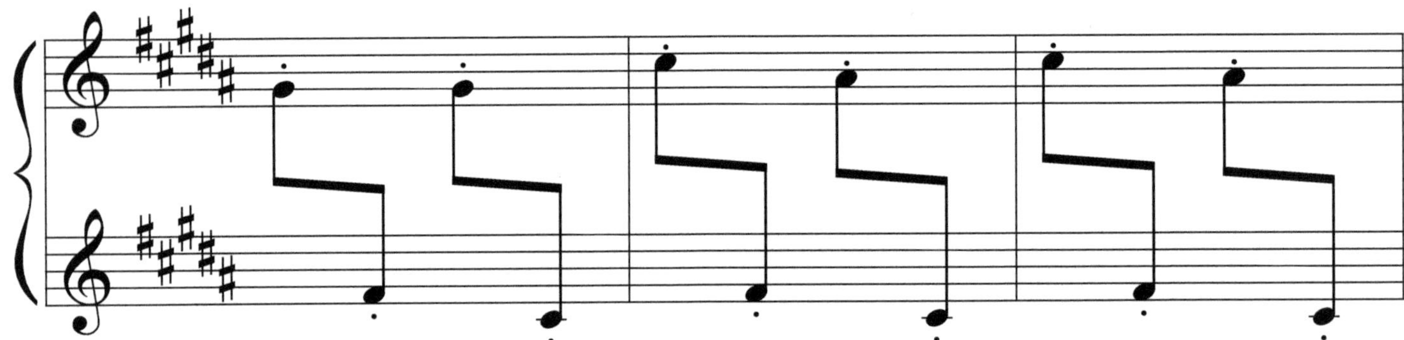

GA 19028

My Dad Got Rid of That Monster under My Bed

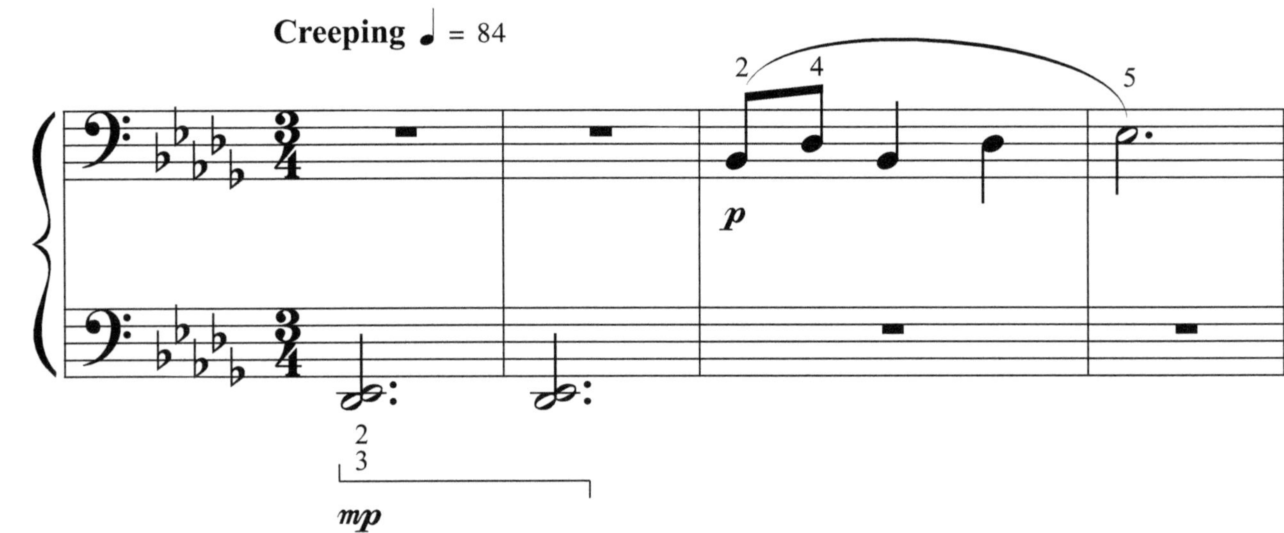

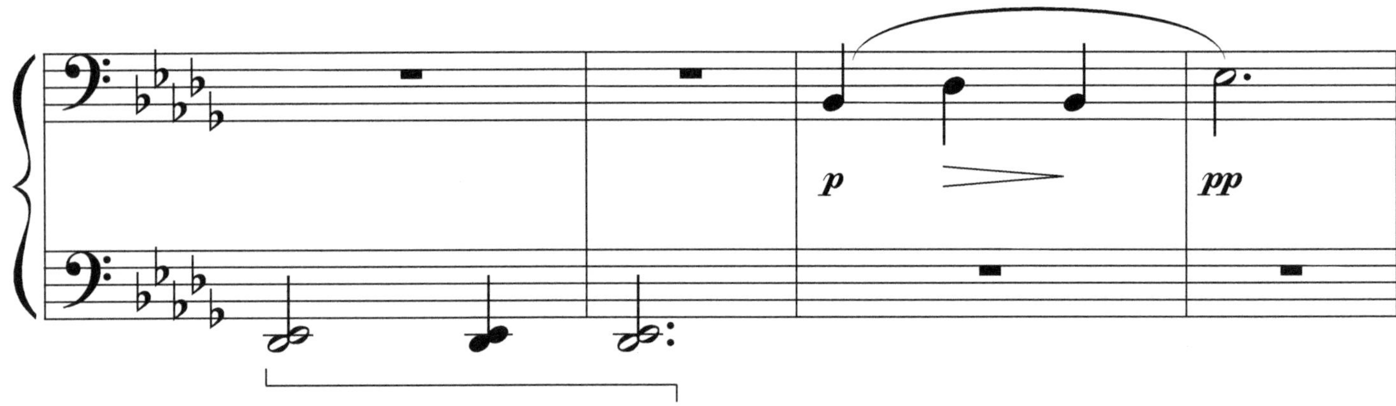

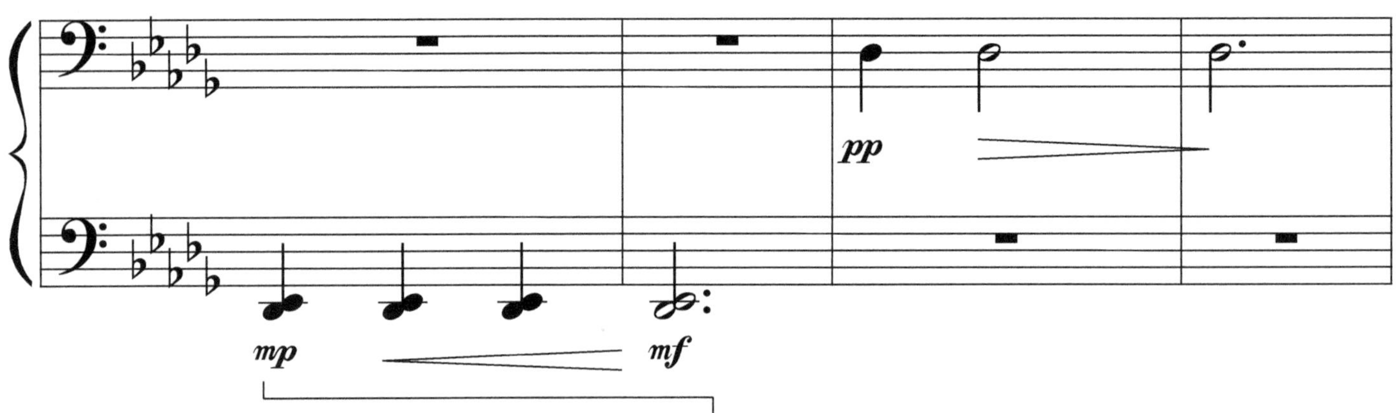

GA 19028

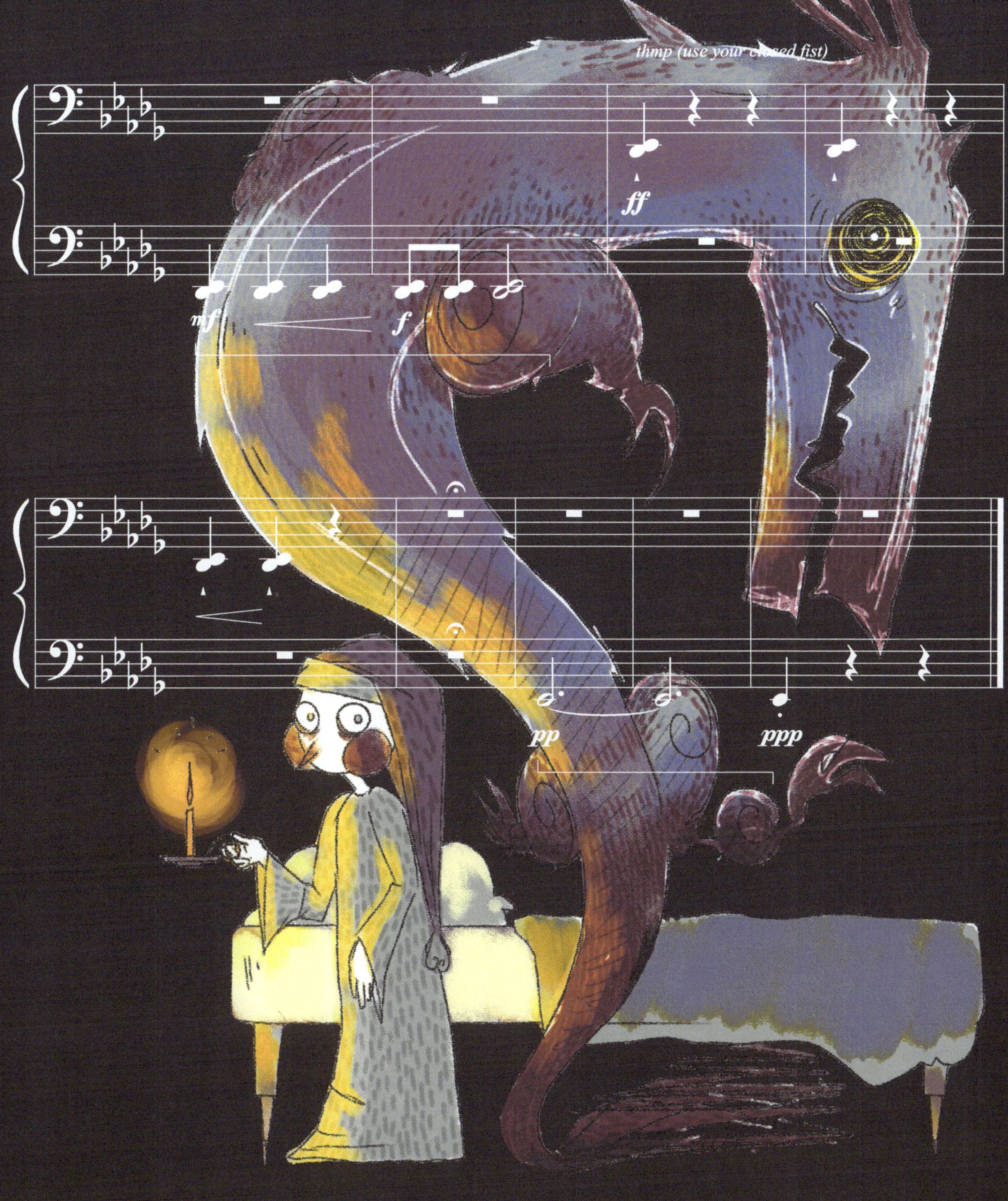
thmp (use your closed fist)
ff
mf
f
pp
ppp

GA 19028

Skipping the Rope

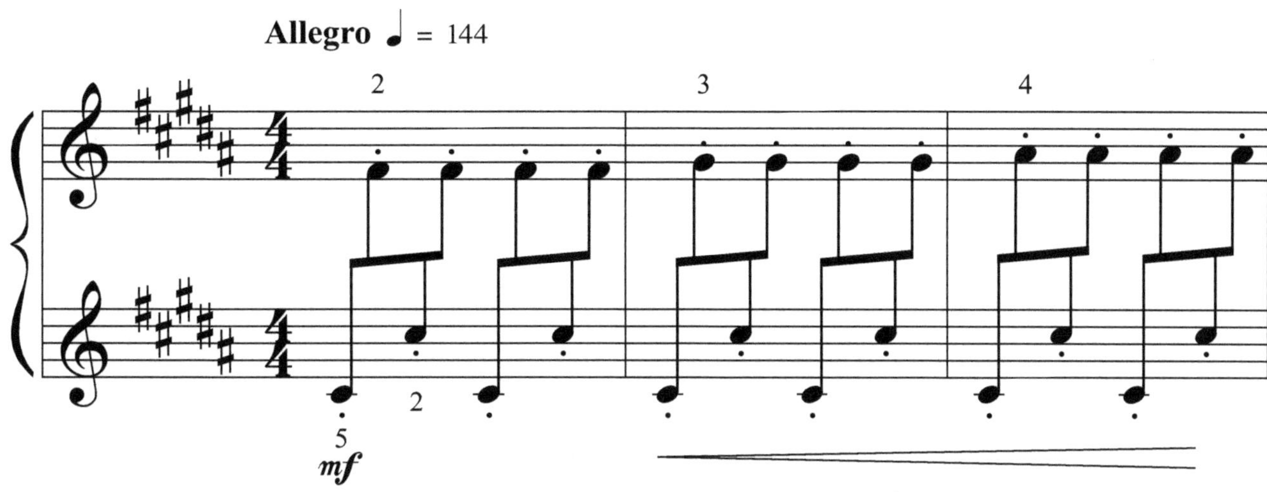

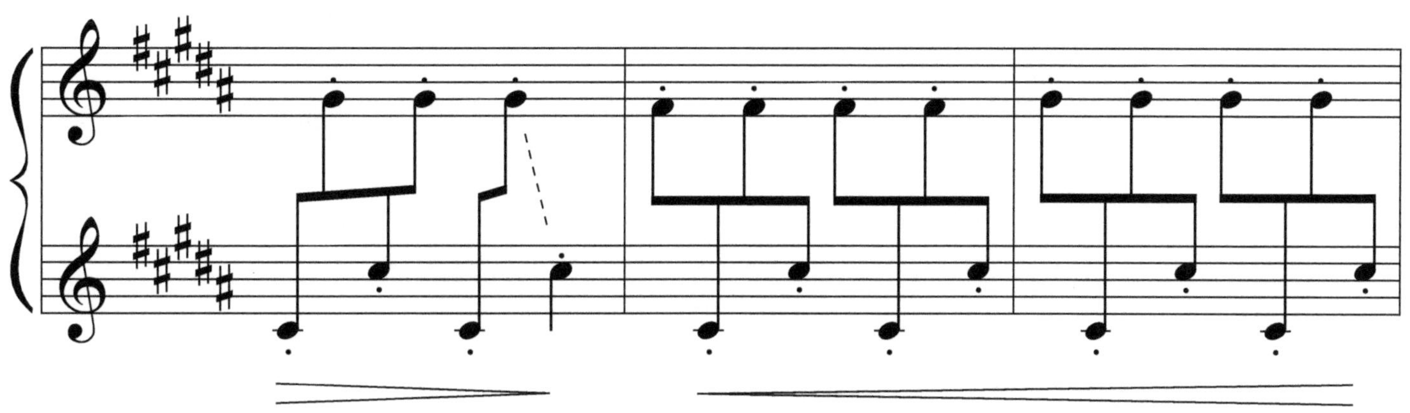

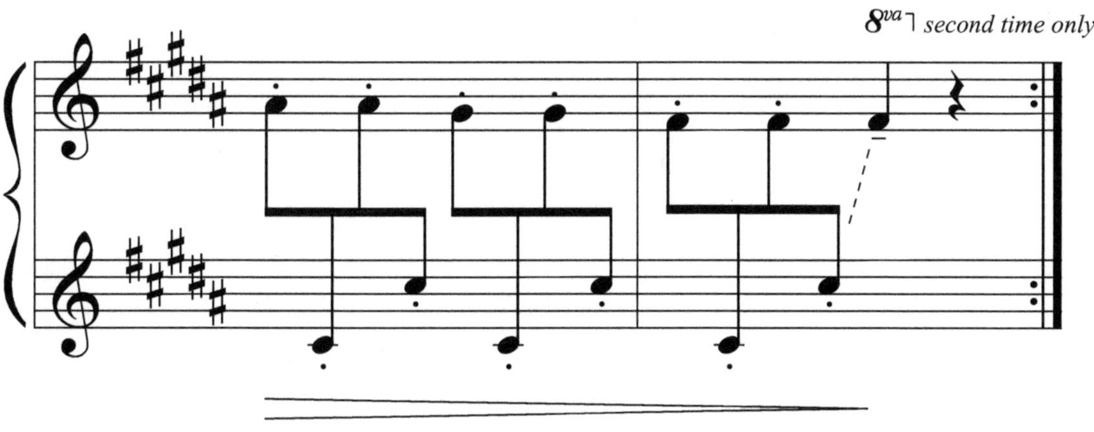

GA 19028

The Magic Island

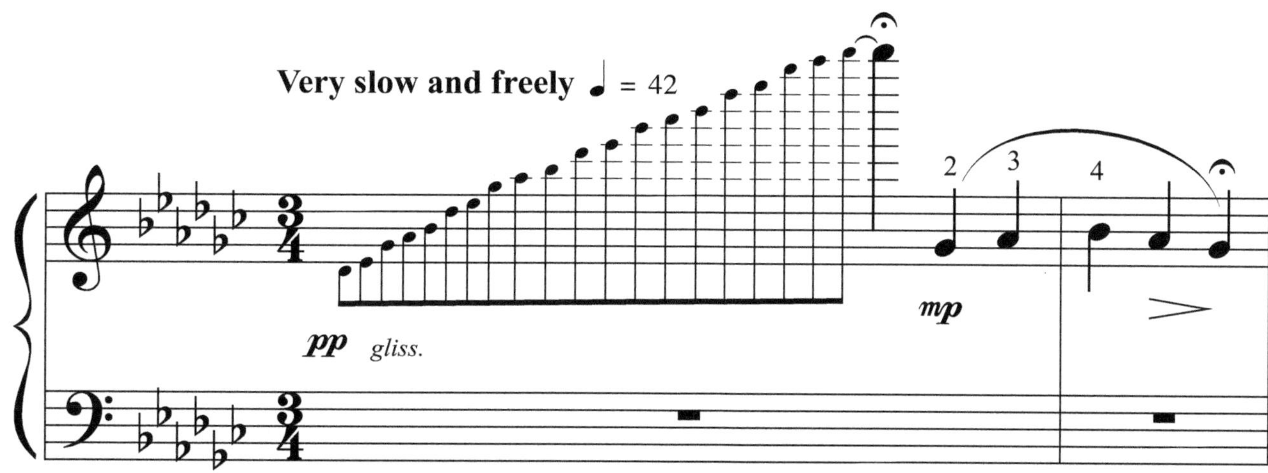

sustain pedal always pressed down

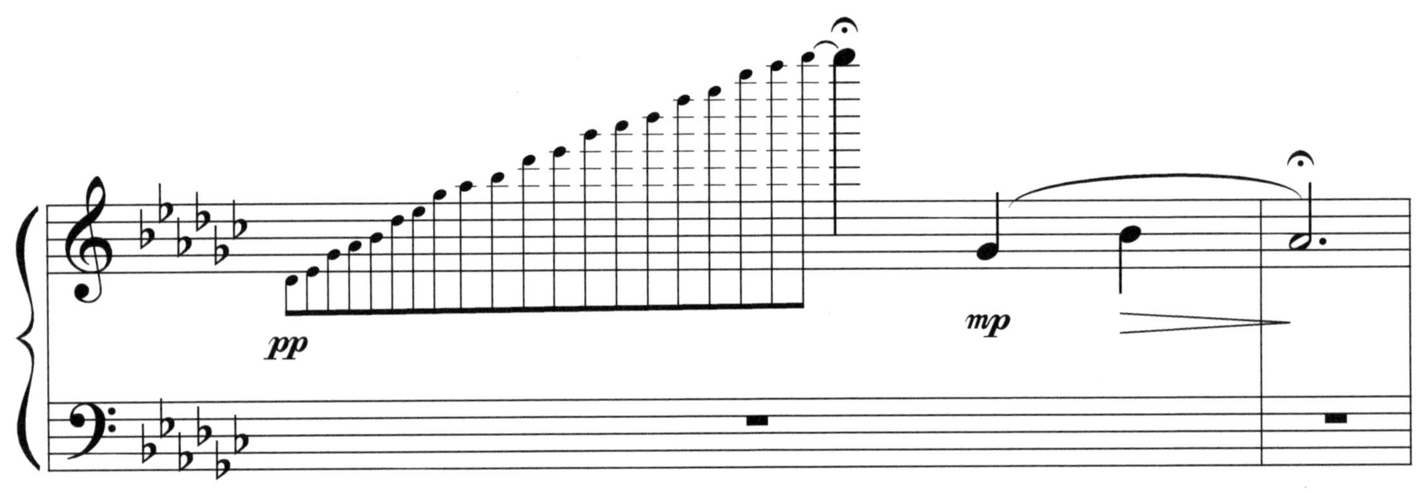
pp
mp

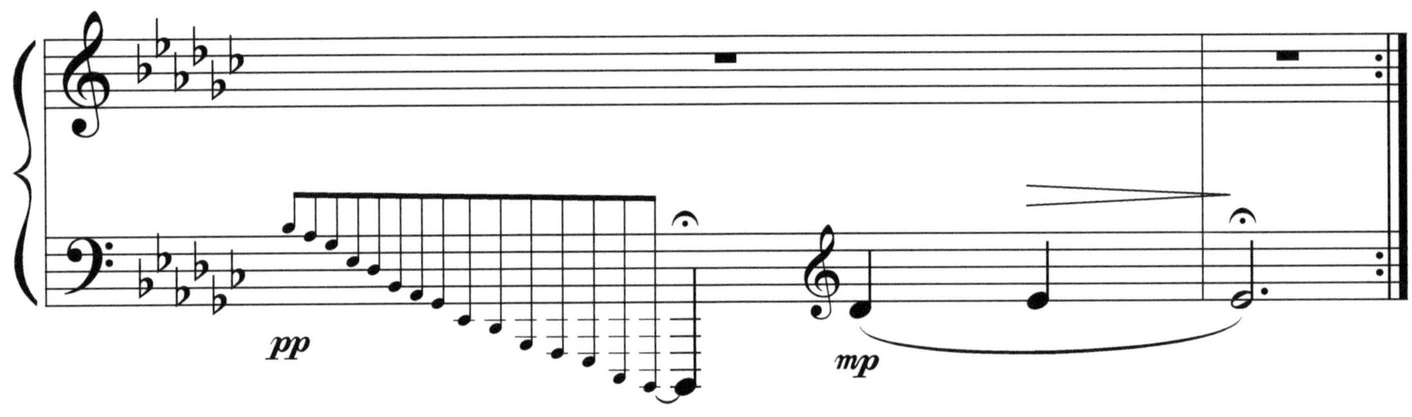
pp
mp

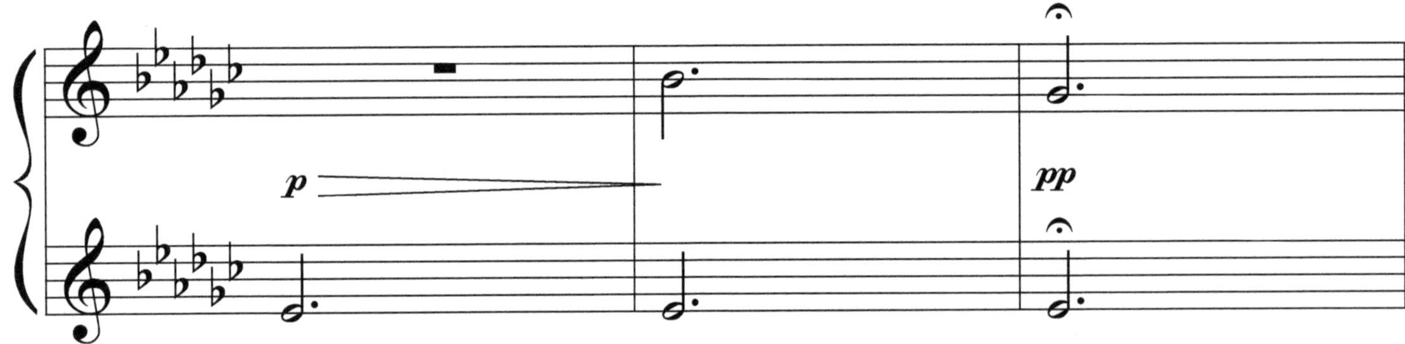
p
pp

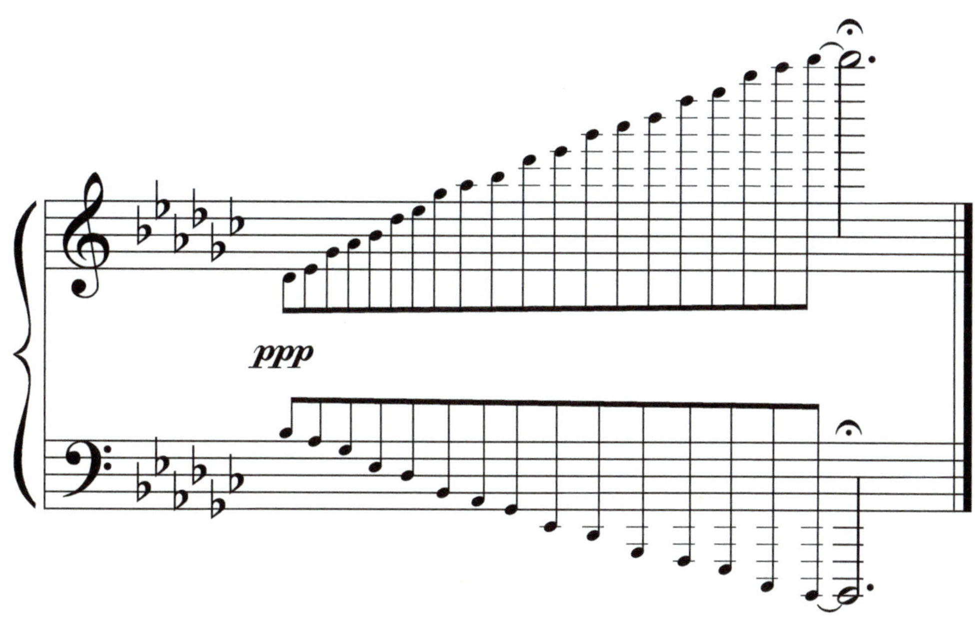

ppp

Lillie, My Little Hamster

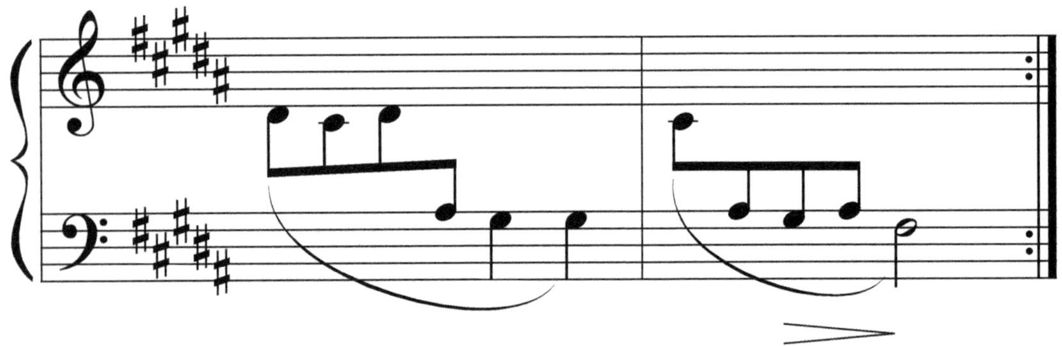

GA 19028

GA 19028

Meditation

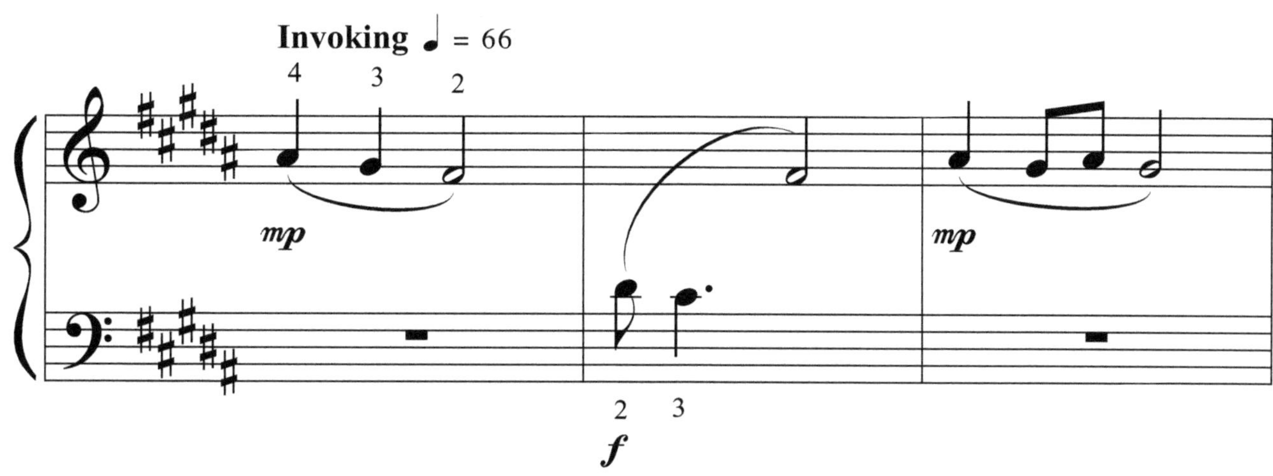

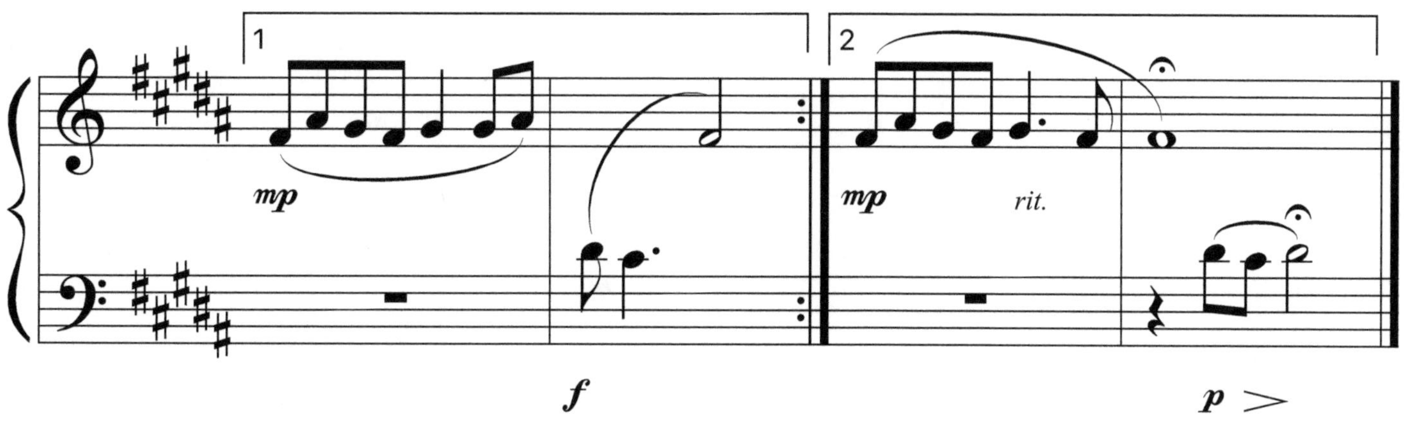

Spock Rock

Steady rock ♩ = 138

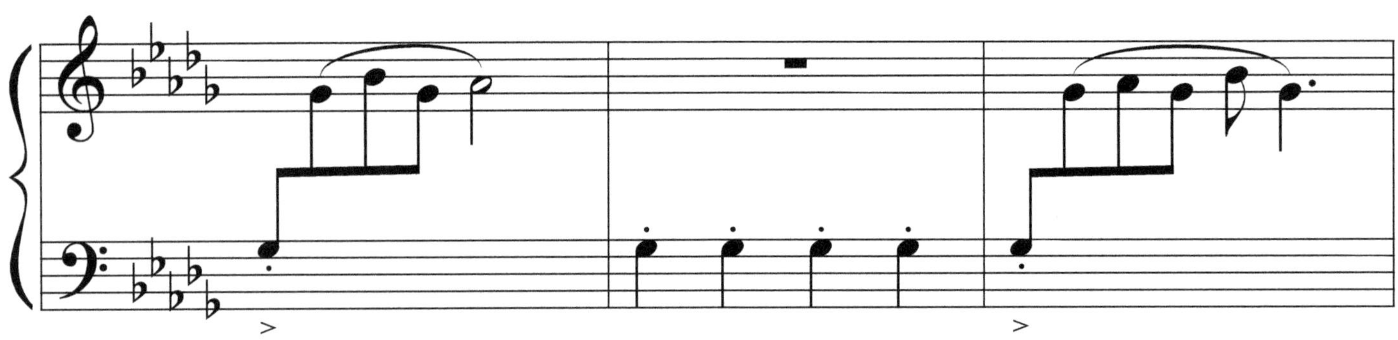

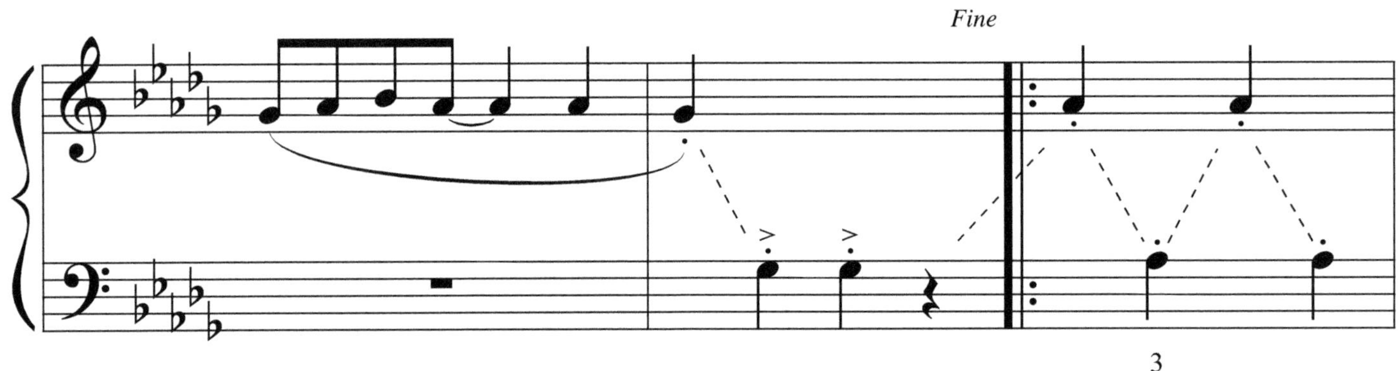

GA 19028

D.C. al Fine
f

Out for a Walk

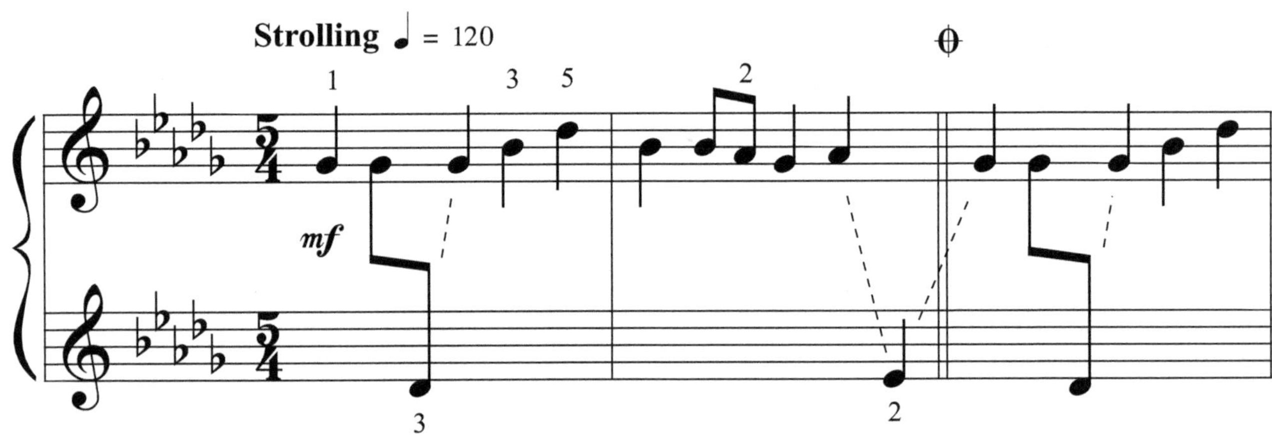

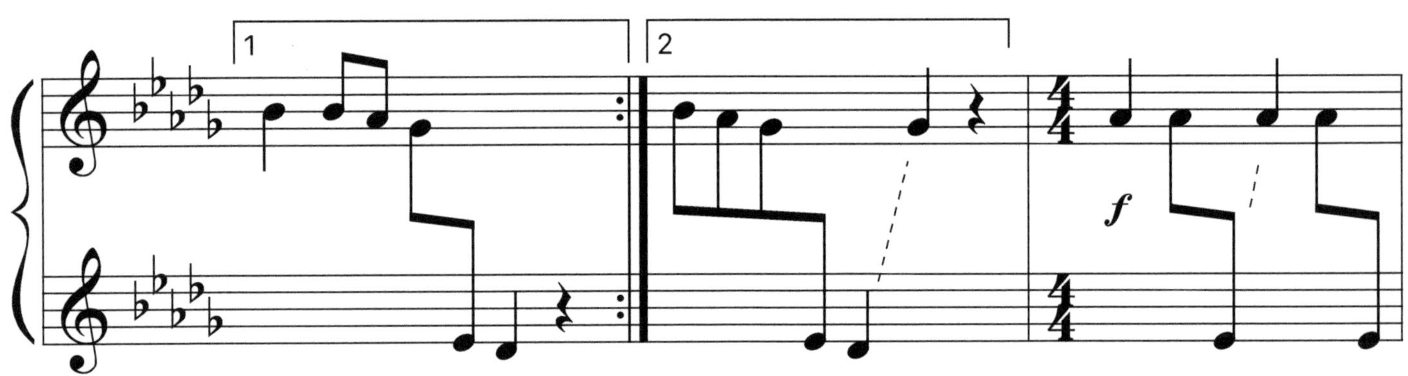

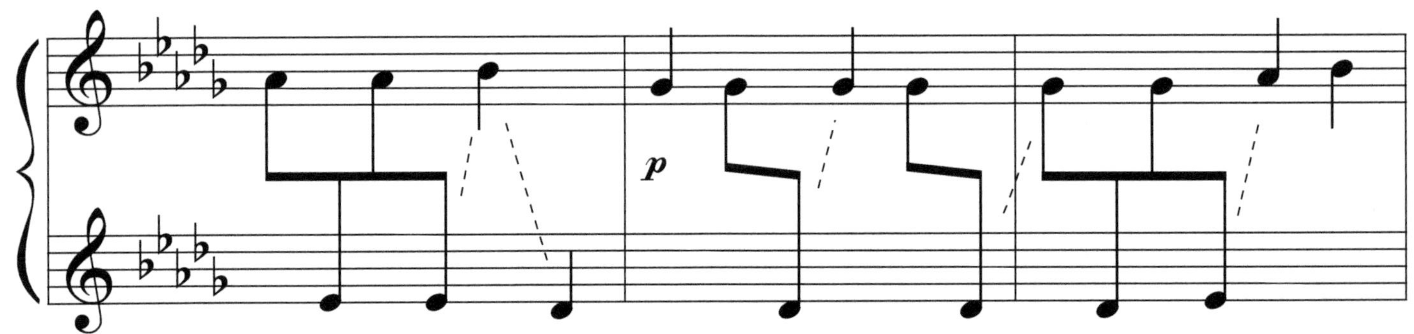

GA 19028

20 Super Easy Piano Pieces on the Black Keys
f
p
D.C. with repeat then D.S. al Coda
Coda
© 2016 - GA music
GA 19028
39

The Chinese Factory

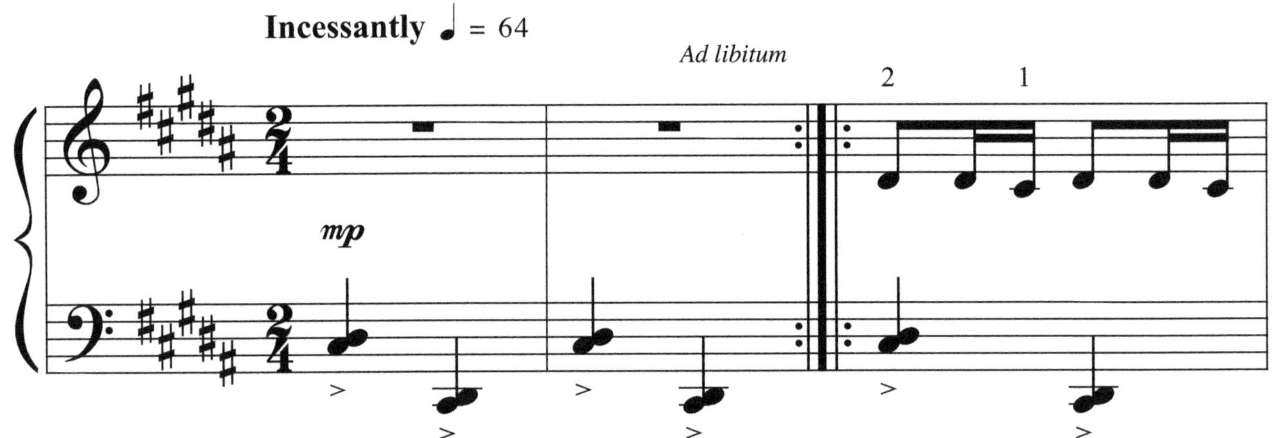

thump the black keys with your fist throughout

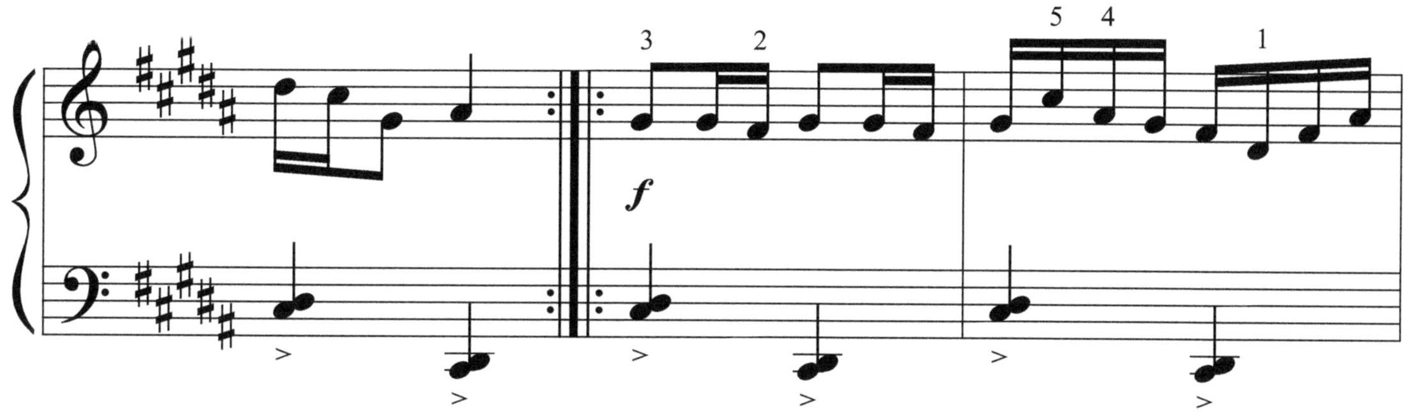

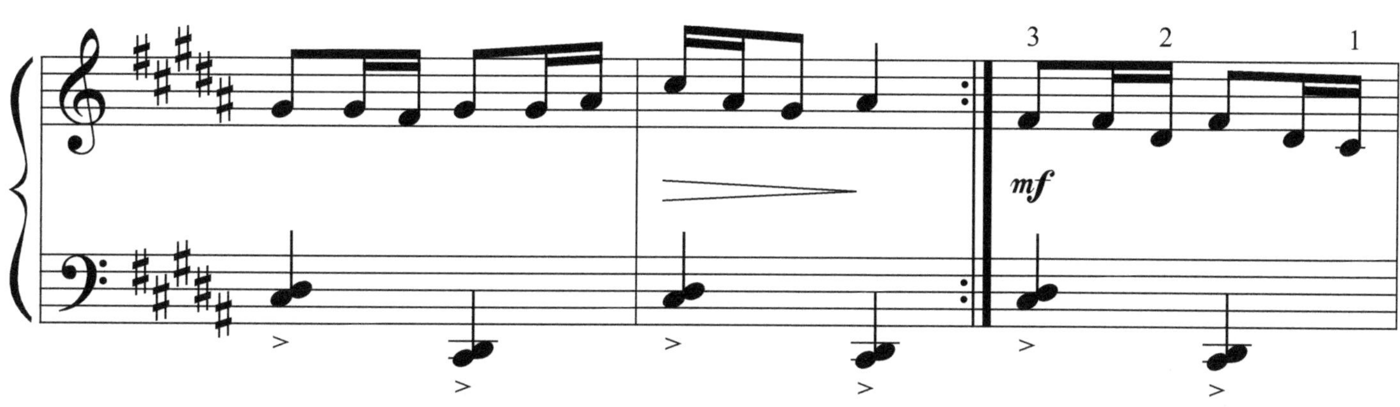

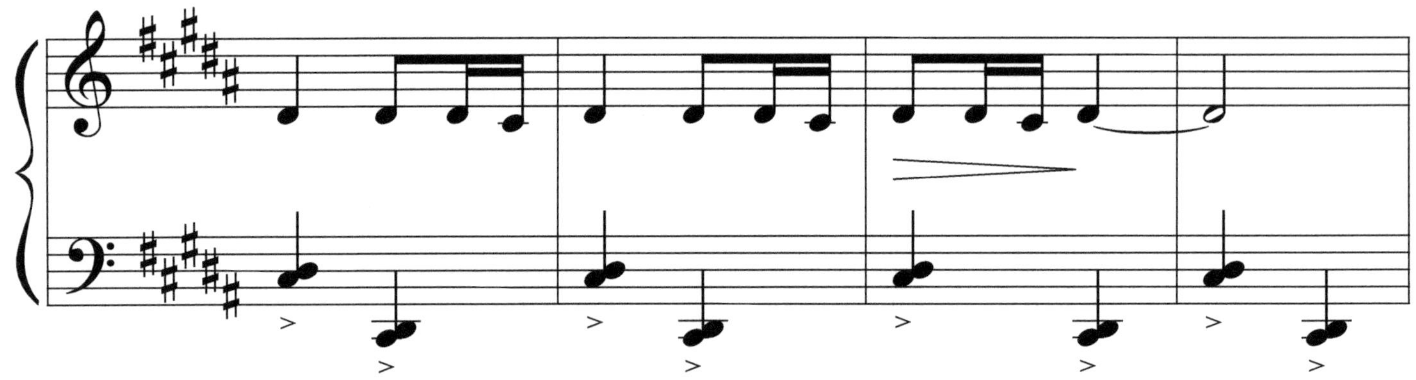

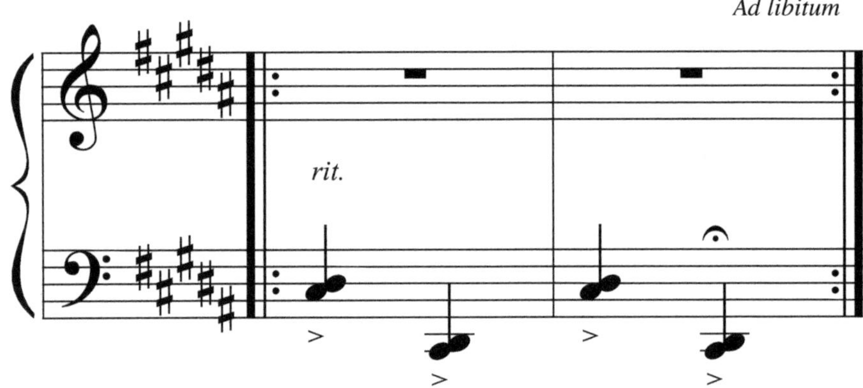

GA 19028

GA 19028

PMP Development Areas

Note Reading
Sing & Play
Listen & Play
Piano Development
Sight Reading
Piano Technical Exercises
Scales & Arpeggios
Études
Quick Studies
Piano Improvisation
Composition
Solo Repertoire
Duet Repertoire
Chamber Music Repertoire